CW00427819

Translated from Russian by Yuri Stepanenko.

The Selected

Sergey Yesenin

The Selected

Contents

1. Dawn's Scarlet Light 1
2. Believe in Happiness 2
3. Don Juan 3
4. I Tire of Living 5
5. Rustling Canes 6
6. Brilliant Star 7
7. Foolish Elation 8
8. Trickling Tears 9
9. A Rascal's Song 10
10. What Is Gone Cannot Be Retrieved 12
11. No Regret 13
12. A Letter to Mother 14
13. Now Everything's Settled 16
14. The Night 18
15. The Blue Flame 19
16. Time's Passage in Your Eyes 20
17. The Still Golden Grove 21
18. You Do Not Love 22
19. Beyond the Mountains 24
20. The Frozen Maple 25
21. The Silver Bluebell 26
22. The Witch 27
23. Don't Look with Such Reproach 28
24. Your Presence and Your Glance 29
25. Sunday Morning 30
26. Your Forced Smile 31
27. I Left My Dearest Land 32
28. Sing of My Life 33
29. To Kluyev 35
30. I Know This Lowly Little House 36

31. The Flowers' Farewell 38
32. The Deception of Life 39
33. My Grief...40
34. I Have Returned Home 41
35. A Shepherd's Life 42
36. Letter to the Woman...43
37. Whit Is the Coat and Red the Sash 46
38. The Snowstorm...47
39. I Won't Sleep 48
40. You Have Been Used 49
41. Would This Be the Last Time 50
42. Blue Is the Night..51
43. The Snow-Clad Plain..52
44. Fall Not, My Little Star.....................................53
45. A Three Horse Sleigh..54
46. My Dear Old House 55
47. Don't Torment Me 56
48. Little House with Light Blue Shutters 57
49. Fields of Wheat That Shine Like Gold at Night....58
50. I Will Not Be Wandering Out............................59
51. Jubilant Adolescence 60
52. With a Humble Heart 61
53. The Gate of Paradise...62
54. My Heart in Its Sorrowful Glory 63
55. My Life 64
56. Farewell, My Friend, Farewell 64

1. Dawn's Scarlet Light

Dawn's scarlet light reflects from the lake,
As the cry of the capercaillie declares it awake.

Hidden in the trees, an oriole replies.
My heart's so light, I do not want to join their cries.

Knowing you will meet me later in the day,
When we will sit down on a fresh bale of hay.

I will caress you, so drunk with the joy,
We will talk so freely, a girl and a boy.

You will succumb to the feeling as I hold you tight
And we will be drunk by the joy through the night.

Let the capercaillie's weeping ring loud and clear.
Our longing sings sweetly for just us to hear.

2. Believe in Happiness

You must believe in happiness!
For the sun is not yet gone
And with dawn's brilliant red
Promises each man to bless.
You must believe in happiness!

Ring, golden Russia, forever.
Oh blow you wind, so unabated.
Blessed are those who have celebrated
Your pastoral sadness and weather.
Ring, golden Russia, forever.

I love to hear the turbulent water.
And see the stars brilliantly shine,
Even on all those who suffer and pine,
The country so blessed, each son, each daughter.
How I love to hear the ever turbulent water.

3. Don Juan

Perhaps later, it may be too early,
I have not thought about it for a long time,
To be like Don Juan, so complete and so surely,
A fickle man immersed in meter and rhyme.

What happened? Why am I compelled
Every day a different woman? How frail!
Discarding all pity, each one I have held,
Immune to jealousy and betrayal.

I have always kept my heart from simple,
Tender feelings, and I wonder,
What do I seek in each smile, each dimple?
What hollow spell am I under?

Contempt, be my blanket and shield.
You have ever marked me.
White hot feelings, to them, I don't yield,
Immersed in cold lilac perpetually.

My heart reflects a lovely lemon sunset
And through the foggy haze of though I hear
"Don Juan, a challenge to accept,
The freedom from love's tender sneer."

Without passion, the challenge is taken,
And not a thing in my life will change.
With tempests of sensations my heart is shaken,
The fake, never real, is all my heart's range.

My story is told. You now know my reason,
Why every day a new woman, without fail.
It is why I can smile through each season,
Immune to jealousy and betrayal.

4. I Tire of Living

I tire of living in a land that's not mine,
Of buckwheat fields pastorally fragrant,
I leave my lone cabin without any sign,
For a life as a thief and a vagrant.

Passing through the white shades of life,
Searching for repose in a miserable dwelling.
My dearest friend plans me for his knife.
What is the reasons? There is no telling.

In spring, the sun reflects on the fields,
Wrapping around a stained yellow path.
The girl to whose name my heart yields,
Will turn me out in her wrath.

Sullen, I return to my father's land,
And watch others happiness bloom.
On fine evening a shirt transform with my hand
To a noose, and I'll hang in my gloom.

The gray willow near the hedge,
With bowed head, will weep in reply.
To dogs barking around on night's edge,
Buried unwashed, in death will I lie.

The moon will return, as ever she does,
Rowing her steady way 'cross the sky.
And Russia will continue with life's buzz,
Dancing and crying with each quarter gone by.

5. Rustling Canes

Rustling canes on the river's wide bank
The princess was crying, her face now is blank.

Where once she chanted "loves me – loves me not,"
The unwoven flowers no more has she sought.

No more will she have her wedding in spring
The forest had secrets, its own wedding ring.

As mice loudly stripped the birch of its bark,
The girl became frightened of the idea of dark.

The horses were restless and fiercely shook their heads
The secrets stepped back from those horses in dread.

Too late, the smell of sweet incense rose
While winds whispered softly a dirge where she froze.

The girl now is waiting alone, the shore all around,
With the foam's golden ring weaving her shroud.

6. Brilliant Star

Oh brilliant star way up high,
How many mysteries do you hold inside?
Not one deep idea do you belie,
What is it about you that inspires far and wide?

You bright stars, so many side by side!
What makes your beauty so strongly alluring?
Heavenly bodies, how can you afford to hide
This craving for learning you are constantly stirring?

And why, little beacon of light,
Do you invite us into your embrace?
Your gentle promises creating delight,
Yet you are too far, buried in space.

7.   Foolish Elation

Now stirs that foolish elation,
The window shows a view of the lawn
To witness the ruby red sunset,
Eloquently crossing the pond like a swan.

Greetings to you golden peace
Reposing in shadow from birch to the water.
The crows congregate under the Evening Star,
Using the roof as their nightly alter.

Somewhere beyond the garden,
Timidly over the bud where it springs
A girl clad in white
A tender song sings.

An elegant gown, the evening sweeps through
Clothing the meadow with a nightly chill.
This foolish elation, such happiness,
Sweeps freshly across my cheeks and my will.

8. Trickling Tears

Your unhidden tears trickled down your cheeks,
And unchecked, they wetted the ground.
As sad and hurt as I was to see them that evening,
To me, their meaning was not to be found

You flew from me then for distant lands,
Leaving all dreams a colorless sheen.
With you now gone, again I'm alone,
No tenderness, a life that is mean.

Frequently, I wander out in the evening,
To places where we used to go.
And as I return, your image awaits me,
The tears again start that last steady flow.

9. A Rascal's Song

I will not deceive myself or another,
The concern sinks deep into my heart.
Why do they call me a cheater, a crook,
Accusing me of playing a brawlers part?

No villain am I, hiding to thieve,
Nor have I harmed an imprisoned man.
I am a simple, idle fellow
Who smiles and smiles, without a plan.

I am a naughty reckless Moscow loner,
Reveling throughout the city, along every street,
And every dog within these walls,
Knows me by my regular, reveling beat.

Each run down horse tied up outside
Gives me a nod in salutation
For I am a good friend to animals,
My verse serves as their medication.

The hat that I don is not for the ladies,
Such turbulent emotions are far to distressing,
I have a far better use for my hat and my time,
The constant joy brought with oats, not caressing.

With people I cannot be friends,
Resigned to another kingdom am I,
With such a strong preference to lend out my tie
To any dog that is standing nearby.

So from this day forth no more will I care
In my heart and my soul a sun shines absolution.
It is why they charge me with crime and dissention,

Their words in my heart will no more be a pollution.

10. What Is Gone Cannot Be Retrieved

As the lovely night I will never know again,
I have held my dear love for the very last time.
The nightingale's song my heart cannot win,
As it sang to us loving, so sweet and sublime!

Claimed by the cold local spring,
You cannot call time back with a plea for delay.
Autumn returns in the seasonal ring,
Paired with the rains, the dirt turned to clay.

In her cold earthen grave, soundly she sleeps,
Storing my love in her heart, as she lives in mine,
Untouched by the blizzard as around her it weeps.
It cannot wake her, of life there's no sign.

The nightingale has ceased in its song,
Not on these shores; it has taken to flight.
No more will it sing to me now that it's gone,
The tender, sweet song we shared on that night.

Flown away too are the joyous emotions,
The experience had me so well deceived.
Too cold is my heart to other commotions;
What is gone cannot be retrieved.

11. No Regret

Feel no regret, remorse, or pain,
As fog rolls by, all things will pass.
So to must I wilt and fade,
'Til youth is gone at last.

Having been touched and cooled by age,
My heart will never again be so inflamed.
The land of the beautiful birch
Can no longer lure my feet so tamed.

Where once my vagabond spirit raced,
It s flow now stifled, it seldom moves me.
I have lost youth's new bloom
No more wild eyed, moved not by spontaneity.

My wild desires no longer bridled.
Is this my life? Or was I merely dreaming?
It is as though I sat astride
A rosy horse and passed youth by unseeing.

We all live in a wilting world
Where copper leaves to earth descend.
May you be ever blessed
In this place where all things end.

12. A Letter to Mother

Are you still with us, mother my dear?
As live and well as I? Here's a hear felt hello.
May you always have evening's honey light
Around your home as a heavenly halo.

I hear that you worry and fret
Thought often dwelling on me
That your anxiety drives you to the road
In a worn overcoat staring unseeingly.

Each evening you spend imagining me
The same sad scene of a wasted life
A bloody bar brawl, a villain descends
And so is my end on the point of a knife.

Dearest, calm down! It isn't real.
You're paining yourself with that dreadful delusion.
You'll see your son is not such a slovenly drunkard.
Take heart and cease this wretched illusion.

I am the same gentle soul,
And my dreams have now turned
From this life that's proved false
For a while it is for home I have yearned.

I'll return with the spring
When the flowers bloom white as the snow
My simple request is to let me sleep,
Don't' wake me early as you did years ago.

And please do not stir or probe
Through dreams or strife I have known
For I learned far too early in life

The heavy burden of dreams futilely sewn.

Please do not teach me to pray!
For I cannot return to that way.
You, my sole hope and comfort,
They constant light I count on today.

So please forget all your fears
You need not fret over me
That your anxiety drives you to the road
In a worn overcoat staring unseeingly.

13. Now Everything's Settled

Now everything's settled, no going back
I am gone form my home
The land of the poplar no more
To serve as my shroud where I roam.

The house is burdened by my departure
And my dog died a long time ago,
But I shall go on in the crooked streets
Of Moscow to live and to die I know.

I cherish this city of elms
Each decrepit building and home
Golden somnolent Asian entities
Repose lightly on each temple dome.

With the moon's light starting to fade,
God knows how it can light the way.
I go in dejection down familiar streets
To the tavern to keep depression at bay.

Through the ruckus and noise in that eerie den
To the moon's ending stages
I recite poems to girls of the night
And carouse with those who steal for their wages.

My heart becomes frenzied
And I utter worthless words
"Just like you, that I am.
You cannot go back after joining this herd!"

The house is burdened by my departure
And my dog died a long time ago,
But I shall go on in the crooked streets

Of Moscow to live and to die I know.

14. The Night

The tired day droops into serene night,
Noise gives way to a still silence
As the sun bids adieu and retires its light,
The moon brings its dreamy opulence.

The valley listens intently
To tender whisperings of the stream
And the night draped forests dream
To the nightingale's lullaby sung so gently

Joined together, an audience
The bank murmurs back and forth with the river
Their quiet talks are hidden
By the reeds that dance and quiver.

15. The Blue Flame

The blue flames having from up above
I forgot my original intention
For now I first can sing of love
I need no fights, no brute contention

I once was like an abandoned garden,
Thriving on fast women and heavy drinking
These things have lost their appeal,
No more do I revel in my heart sinking.

For no it is my single desire
To gaze into your gold-brown eyes.
There as you see my heart's fire
All thought of others from you flies.

Oh gentle step of one so graceful,
If you only knew this obstinate heart,
A man who has been so rebellious and wasteful,
He still can love and play loves part.

I would forever forgo reveling, drunken bands
And poetry I can stop writing without a care,
Only to touch your tender hands
And caress your wavy auburn hair.

Forever together, like a hand and glove,
Wherever you go, I'll be in your retention.
For now I first can sing of love
I need no fights, no brute contention

16. Time's Passage in Your Eyes

I am so sad to look on you
For it brings pain and pity too
Knowing all we have is what we remember
This time of life a willowy September.

By other lips your are all worn,
Your warmth and body torn.
So like the drizzle of the rain,
The soul is numbing to the pain.

Well, I shall not be bound by fear,
For so much happiness I've known here
That nothing can remain
Only dampness and decay to gain.

I could never steal myself
To a quite, smiling settled shelf,
So few roads travelled down
Yet for so many errs be renowned.

How funny this chaotic life I fill with laughter
So it has been and it will be ever after.
The grove so full of birch-tree bones
It's like a graveyard's whispered moans.

Likewise we head to our end
To fade like callers to the garden,
Since winter lacks the colored flowers
Grief of them should not be ours.

17. The Still Golden Grove

The golden grove is now still:
Before the birch, alive with idle chatter,
The sullen cranes fly over with graceful skill;
I regret no more, it does not matter.

Who is left to pity? They are all travelers
They come and go, return and leave again
The moon and hempen bush above the water
Remember all who perished filled with pain

I stood alone in that open spot,
Watching the winds taking the cranes.
I thought of my youth now shot,
Yet of regret I felt no pangs.

Pity no my wasted years
For I've no sorrow in my lilac should
The purple rowan burning in the garden
Brings no warmth or comfort with its toll.

The rowan will keep its color
Heat touched grass will not die
As a tree drops leaves so quietly
So do my sorrowful words fly.

18. You Do Not Love

You do not love or feel from me compassion.
Am I not considerably handsome?
Looking away you are filled with passion,
Resting your arms on me, my ransom.

You are so young, so sensitive, so pleasing.
My influence for you is neither good nor bad.
How many men have you petted while teasing?
How many kissed, how many you have had?

I know for you now they are merely shadows,
Always leaving you still inflamed.
So many laps have been your hallows
As you now sit in mine so unashamed.

Though your eyes are half closed with me
Your thoughts have strayed on to another.
And because I feel the love as equally,
I prefer to think on a better discover.

Don't call this zeal predestination,
Such hasty ties are worthless and worn.
Surely you know this is an unplanned connection,
Happily I leave you, I will not leave torn.

Yes, and you too will go wherever you please
In continued thoughts, wasting ways.
But those too young, do not seize,
Those unscathed, leave them alone to happier days.

When you walk about with someone else
Gushing meaningless words of love with him,
Perhaps I will be out walking myself,

And shall encounter your smile once again.

Turning away you look at me grinning
And bend yourself slightly forward like this,
You whisper quite softly "Good evening."
An I answer back to you "Good evening, miss."

None of this will touch my heart
Not one bit of it will give me pain.
He who has once been in love is smart,
For he will never really love again.

19. Beyond the Mountains

Beyond the mountains and yellow fields
Rests a village whose drowsy arms
Stretch out toward the woods where it yields
The ivy draped fences containing it charms.
It is there, above the steeples' tops
Morning rises a misty heaven blue
And the wind wisps tiny water drops
Across the grass the lake's own dew.

It is not the spring like valley song
That always draws me to this place
But like a crane, I yearn and long
To the hilltop convent to turn my face.

Each evening as the blue sky blurs
And behind the bridge the weary sun strays
Religiously my solemn pilgrim stirs
And draws with love before the cross to prey.

Chaste is live in this holy land
As life and prayer are one in the same
Please pray you now with claspèd hands
For this lost soul with only himself to blame.

20. The Frozen Maple

Oh my dear maple, frozen in ice
Do you five in? Is the blizzard your vice?

Have you seen visions or heard rumors today,
Like you would have on a stroll in sweet may?

Like an intoxicated officer out on a beat,
Caught in a show drift, too drunk on your feet.

I myself am prone to such misdirection
After reveling late I know not my home section.

Staggering home I catch glimpses of several trees
In the blizzard I sing to them of a summer breeze.

And I know I am most like a maple,
Not one in winter's grip, but one living in April.

Leaving modesty behind, so much like a louse,
I would hug a birch like somebody's spouse.

21. The Silver Bluebell

Silver bluebell, how do you sing!
Or is my heart soundly dreaming?
Light from a rosy icon flashes
Falling on my golden lashes.

Though no longer a sweet little boy
Joying in the pigeon's splashing
My dreams are kind and happy
Through new forests, racing, dashing.

I do no need the narrow house
Nor find delight in word or mystery.
What I seek, I hope you teach me.
No more to wake, this life my history.

22. The Witch

Deathly white, terribly unkempt, she appears outrageous,
Running, rushing, playing so courageous.

The dark night fears this bout of silence
As the clouds cover the new moon hence.

The wind sings in fevered howls
Rushing into the wild wood's bowels.

Fir-trees threaten with tips like spears,
Owls screech and wail to express their fears.

Waving skeletal arms the bony witch shouts,
Behind the clouds stars fear to come out.

Snake like ringlets drape round her face,
As blizzard-like she whirls round in place.

In the ringing of a pine the witch dances and cries,
Clouds grow dark in trepidation as they pass by.

23. Don't Look with Such Reproach

Don't look at me with such reproach
Malice toward you I do not bear
But I like your look as you approach
And your feigned modesty as you stand there.

While you seem so openhearted,
I would be rather pleased to see
How a fox after pretending it has departed
Catches crows, as you intend to catch me.

Try to catch me, I won't be daunted
Keep that ardor of yours unrestrained
So many like you my person have haunted,
Flailing to keep my heart as it waned.

It is not you that I love so dearly,
You are merely a living ghostly shade.
I desire another to stay by me yearly,
A lovely, doll-like blue-eyed maid.

Though she doesn't act humble
And at first is unnaturally cool,
Her majestic gait without stumble
Rekindles perpetual love from my soul.

No, she is not one to be cheated.
Whatever you are, she is desire
In my heart you can be easily deleted
Your wiles and plans don't stir such a fire.

Indeed, I scorn you, yet act the layman,
So shy and open to you I say,
Whatever the existence of a hell or a heaven,
If they are not, men makes them anyway.

24. Your Presence and Your Glance

Let us sit down side by side
And in our eyes love that we bare
I want to see within your gentle glance
The sensual blizzard you keep in there.

The golden autumn
And fair lock of hair
Have come like salvation
To the rebel free from care

Long ago I left my home
Of blooming fields and thickets
Drawn to the city I went alone
But the dream is bitter and wicked.

I yearned to have an artist's heart
Spending golden days of summer in that garden
The frog's song inspired in part
The blossoming of my poetic self then.

Autumn with the golden branches
Maple and lime trees taking pleasure
Using twigs, they take their chances,
To reach someone they think a treasure.

These people no longer dwell here,
But we can go to visit them
Inside the churchyard marked by crosses.
Some day here we will eternally rest each limb.

Travelling through our troubles wholly
We shall go like this to the sky.
All winding road are only
For the living traveled by.

Let us sit down side by side
And in our eyes love that we bare
I want to see within your gentle glance
The sensual blizzard you keep in there.

25. Sunday Morning

Sunday morning is time for Trinity devotion
The groves white birches ring and sway in motion.

The villagers wake from the festive sleep and come
To the gospel. Drunk with the Spring, they hum.

The window shows blooming tree branches,
At church with new flowers I weep for my chances.

The birds sing near a doleful song,
I bury my youth as a I sing along.

Sunday morning is time for Trinity devotion
The groves white birches ring and sway in motion.

26. Your Forced Smile

Don't force that smile upon your lips
For another girl my heart does flips.

As you already know, and you know it well,
That I'm here for someone else, I need not tell.

Simply by change, not because I care,
I passed this way and stopped just to stare.

27. I Left My Dearest Land

It is true, I left my dearest land
Left my Russia of clear blue
Under the birch by the pond in the sand
My mother's sorrow rekindled anew.

Like a golden frog, the moon descends
And across the water it will sprawl.
Like an apple blossom with grizzled ends,
My father's beard receives tears that fall.

I will not soon, no, not soon return,
Through blizzards I will gladly sing,
While maples protect my Russian land,
Standing alone is their only thing.

I know the joy for all of those
Who have the chance to kiss leaved in the rain.
For the maple and I, we are quite alike,
In the head and the heart, we are plain.

28. Sing of My Life

Sing the same to that cursed guitar, sing,
Strumming your fingers in a wide semicircle.
I am awash in the fumes of the thing,
My last, my only friend, you comfort and encircle.

Do not look at her wrist so divine,
Or the flowers shawl draped 'round her head.
For joy I was looking with this woman to find
But my own perdition I found instead.

I knew not love was a horrid infection.
I knew not love was a wretched plague.
She simply came, and feigned affection,
Driving this ruffian mad while she played.

Sing, my friend. It takes me to better times,
To our early days when she was best.
But let her kiss and pet and fondle others,
The deliciously gorgeous female mess.

Oh wait. I did not choose to curse.
Oh wait. I did not dare to swear.
Let me sing of myself in a verse,
Under the bass string my song will fill the air.

The vault of my days does flow.
And yet I have my golden dreams
I did myself so many women know,
Hugged and held, so many it seems.

Yes! It is one of the world's bitter truths.
As a child I saw it was so, each heart beat,
When the pack of dogs bared each tooth,
To have the bitch who was in heat.

So why am feel so jealous within my head?
Why do I let it cause such pain?
Our life – it was confined to a bed.
Our life – a simple kiss in a pool of strain.

Sing well! Sing! In that fateful sphere,
Of these hands is a well-known end.
Only you know, send them far from here.
I shall not die, not ever, my friend.

29. To Kluyev

Now my love is no more the same.
You too feel the change of situation.
The moon's sweeper could not tame,
Nor make the pools of poetic creation

Though sad, you rejoice at the star
That bends and falls upon your eyes.
Though scattered around the house so far,
Within your heart no house does lie.

And the one you waited for through the nights,
As before, as passed your home by.
My friend, for whom did you make that key,
Wrought with the gold of your lullaby?

You do not sing about the sun,
And never saw the Heaven's bound.
Like the mill wings flapping as they're spun,
You'll never tear from off the ground.

30. I Know This Lowly Little House

This is a familiar, lowly, little hour,
Crossing the street, I feel so at home,
Across the window rise blue straws of wires,
Weight it down as they have always done.

They years have brought austere contingency,
Bending and beating and blustering through,
Yet it is still the village of my infancy,
And the country still lively in green and blue.

I never sought for fame or contentment,
For I know the vanity of glory and prominence.
Sleeping now, I dream of life devoid of resentment,
A tranquil life at my home exerts its dominance.

The garden sparkles in its vivid blues
And quiet August reclines on the fences.
After circling, birds find lime-trees to use
And in bird bathes their feathers they rinse.

Always I've been fond of the house made of wood.
The logs flashing and showing formidable powers,
Strange howls our stove made when it could
As we stoked the fire in our comfortable bower.

Its wailing louder than a funeral bell,
It's sorrowful as if in mourning.
What could he have seen, this mason's camel,
In the pouring, wailing, drenching rain?

Obviously he saw some foreign bounds
And dreamed of a more flowering phase,
Like the golden Afghanistan grounds
And Bukhara's glassy haze.

So well do I know such locations
I've travelled far to many places.
Now I only want to visit destinations
Close to my home of familiar faces.

Those dreams are now all faded,
They are gone in a smoky blued decay.
Peace be yours, grasses now belated.
Peace be yours, the home where I once played

31. The Flowers' Farewell

The flowers bid adieu to me,
Their heads drooping so far down.
A sign that I will never again see
Her beloved face or this dear town.

So it is the world's way, my dear.
As once I saw the in habitation,,
So too shall I see them in trepidation
With tenderness I accept the complication.

This I've learned each passing day
I've lived my life in a smiling torrent.
Thus to every moment say
The mortal realm is all recurrent.

Some day some one new will come,
But no grief will mend what's past.
He may make a better song,
To the one for whom my heart could not last.

And, with disregard she hears the song,
Caressing her endeared lover's arm,
She may happen to remember love's throng
That flowed from me, a rare flower with my charm.

32. The Deception of Life

Life's a fraud dangling a hypnotic pathos,
There in is its charm and power.
From there it writes with each passing hour
Deceptive letters with hands we loath.

Closing my eyes I silently declare:
Just touch your heart and you will know
Life is deceptive. You must beware
Of promises that draw you so.

Now turn and look upon the sky,
The moon looks back, replying as you plead,
Calm down, mortal, don't rely
On universal claims that you don't need.

It is nice to contemplate spring in a blizzard,
To believe life takes a more friendly way,
Allow a treacherous girl your reputation to mar
And keep a blind eye to friends who betray.

Any girl may love and caress me
Cruel tongues may be razor sharp,
My life has prepared me for bitter contention,
I'm accustomed to their wretched part.

These heights numb my heart, and I'm daunted,
The stars no more produce their lovely, bright fire
Disappointed are those whose love once I flaunted
Forgotten now, they'll ne'er again visit at my door.

Pressed now by such persecution,
I smile, regardless of my epic fall.
Experiencing this world that's so fair
To this life I'm grateful for it all.

33. My Grief

My sorrow will no more be spilt by ringing,
The laughter of bygone days could not last
The lime-tree blossom fades with singing
Though the nightingale's dawns are now passed.

To me it was new in earlier ages
Emotions sweetly filled my heart:
Now words mean naught, no longer contagious,
Taking more of a bitter, rotten part.

Familiar valleys once so wide
No longer appear lovely as before.
The gullies, rolling lands, no longer hide
The disenchantment that's found me forever.

Fading, decaying, rotting, dreary
The sickly pond is torment to the eye.
Yet still I love it all dearly,
I love these visions, even as they make me cry.

The small, rickety house,
The bleat of sheep on the blowing winds,
And the aging horse put out to browse,
Tail waving sadly, his head he bends.

This is our motherland, it is ours,
And though it saddens us in it way,
And draws sobs with its gentle showers,
There is an eternal hope of a joyous day.

Thus my grief can't be spilt by the ringing
The happy laugh of the bygone last.
The lime-tree blossom fades with singing
Though the nightingale's dawns have past.

My sorrow will no more be spilt by ringing,
The laughter of bygone days could not last
The lime-tree blossom fades with singing
Though the nightingale's dawns are now passed.

34. I Have Returned Home

I have returned home to my dear land.
It remains pensive, and gentle around
Pouring gloom with its snow-covered hand
The hill waves hello, friendly low-lying mound.

The drizzle of a cloudy day
Floats over my home all disheveled.
And filled with sadness and dismay,
It is this worry by which I'm now leveled.

Clearing the church's proud dome
The sun a hiding place has found.
My fellow revelers, I have gone home,
And will no more see you around.

The years has dissolved in a whirl.
Where are my friends? Where do they wander?
Listening to the water's gentle purl
Sitting alone it is here I ponder.

I often recline by the hearth.
Hearing the crackling of the broken reeds,
I pray to the warm womanly early
For those forever lost, who ne'er more have needs.

35. A Shepherd's Life

You see here a shepherd, and my parlours
Are new, grassy pastures so ripe,
With rolling, vivacious slopes and furrows
Balks, to the majestic wail of the snipes.

The fluffy, floating clouds are teeming,
As they pass by in lacy designs,
In quiet contemplation I lie dreaming,
And listen to the whisper of pines.

The gentle swaying of dew covered poplars
Sparkle vitality and add to the scene.
As a shepherd, this is my dwelling,
An emerald field, so vibrantly green

Cows salute and welcome me,
Nodding their heads in greeting.
The blooming flowers sell so inviting,
Growing far and at the river meeting.

It is here I forget all worrisome cares
Reclined on softened branches I dream.
Here with the dawn, I whisper my prayers
And in the stillness take communion at the stream.

36. Letter to the Woman

You remember,
Of course you remember,
How I listened
As I stood near the wall.
Anxiously pacing about the chamber,
You sharply reproved me
The bitter words you let fall.

You said
It was time for our parting,
And that my reckless life
Was too much an ordeal,
It was a new life you were starting
While I was fated
To continue to fall downhill.

My sweet!
You did not care for me, I found.
You did not know that my life
Was like a race horse, full of strife,
By a heartless rider beaten round.

You knew it not
That I was immersed in-smoke,
And life was to me flipped upside down.
On misery it was that I was broke,
Because I never saw where we were bound.

Facing each other
We cannot see our place.
We should observe before reaching such perdition.
When boiling oceans invade a ship's space,
That ship is in a deplorable condition.

This world is a ship!
In one felled movement,
Someone searching for a life of glory,
Turns to the thick of storms for improvement
And rides majestically, as in a story.

Well, who
Aboard a majestic boat
Has not fallen, vomited, or cursed?
There are so few who can learn to float
Once despair makes them ready to burst.

Then I
Surrounded by the loud noise,
When so well how I was poised.
Headed down to the ship's hold,
No more to hear or vomiting behold.

That hold
Was a Russian pub
Drowning in the tavern glass,
I found some peace in this loud hub,
Hope that worries would finally pass

My sweet!
How I tormented you.
In tired eyes you showed dejection,
I never tried to hide what was true,
And my life was fraught with altercation

You knew it not
That I was immersed in-smoke,
And life was to me flipped upside down.
On misery it was
That I was broke,
Because I never saw where we were bound.

....

Now many years have passed,
Youth is not with me today.
My feelings changed, new ideas and fears.
Standing at this lavish feast I say
Praise to those who this life can steer.

Today I,
Encouraged by tenderness
With thoughts of you my heart will mend,
Must tell you of such weariness
What I was
And events that have happened.

My sweet,
I'm glad to tell of my surrender.
I escaped from such a wretched fall, and
You see before you on Soviet land
An ardent supporter and defender.

I'm not the man
I used to be.
No more to you am I a threat,
Will not cause such pain today
And I would follow Labour, my pet,
To the English Channel, go where it may.

Please forgive me,
I know you too are changed.
You live
With an intelligent, good man;
You need this not in the life you have arranged,
And I myself am no more in that plan.

Live your life
Lead by your lucky star
Under the tent of fern so kind.
To you I give my warm regard,
Know you're always on my mind,
Yours, faithfully,
        S e r g e y   Y e s e n i n.

37. Whit Is the Coat and Red the Sash

White is the coat and red the sash,
Picking the poppies, I think of the past.
With the sound of the village song,
There I know she is singing along.

I remember her cry upon entering the hut:
"so handsome, but it is not my heart you want
Your burning wind whip through your curls,
But my eyes are now by someone else open."

It is with humbleness I think how she dislikes me.
I danced and drank les than the rest. SO stubbornly,
I stood to the side, most miserable and sad,
Watching the others, drinking and dancing like mad.

That man is lucky, how he feels little shame,
His beard will tickle her as she whispers his name.
The joined in the ring of the dance with such grace,
Her laugher and joy a cruel slap in the face.

White is the coat and red the sash,
Picking the poppies, I think of the past.
With the sound of the village song,
There I know she is singing along.

38. The Snowstorm

The snowstorm wails like a Romany violin cries.
My sweet girl's wicked smile reaches her eyes.

They are so blue, do they give me a scare?
Though great is my need, I can't truly care.

So similar yet vastly contrasted –
You're fresh, I'm wilting, but together we're casted.

I say happy are the young because I am wizened,
Recollecting my early days in age's terrible blizzard.

I do not flatter, the storm is my violin when pinning.
My heart is stone cold as I look at you smiling.

39. I Won't Sleep

What a night! I won't sleep.
The sky aglow as I've never seen
It seems that deep within I keep
The life when I was young and lean.

Foolish, friendly years gone by
Speak not of the game of love and affection.
Better to bask in the moonlit night,
Here in my happier state of reflection.

Let the moon glance down from above
And see my features looking so sadly
As I reflect that there's no way to fall out of love.
And so we see now, you will never love me.

To us all love comes only once,
Leaving you to me so alien. Strangely,
Like a lime tree, with roots in the snow,
Trying to attract us, though vainly.

We both know it all too well
Seeing now at such a late hour
The blue frost and snow that fell
And lack the glory of a flower

We passed through love, our time and day
Now grasping to have someone to admire,
Yet fated as we are today,
We play at love and desire.

Come close, to caress and be embraced tight,
An impassioned kiss, heartless fervour,
My heart dream of May's brilliant light,
A tender love to last me forever.

40. You Have Been Used

Forget that you've been held by another,
For here there is something good still left:
Your shining hair does cast its spell,
Your autumnal, weary eyes look bereft.

Oh age of fall! Well have I known
How expensive is the summer of life
But in this age is better poetry sown,
For it bears more love and known strife.

From my heart I do not lie
And to silly jeers of ostentation
I speak lacking hesitation:
Farewell to rebellious inclination.

Cease right now this trivial trick
I've been so stubborn, but will no more.
My heart has found a sobering of drink
To enliven the heart and soul.

To stalwart September's knocks on my pane
And glancing upon ivy's crimson hue,
I ready myself for this age's reign,
For youth must now take its due.

My forbearance and patience have grown,
I feel a relief from strife and from stress.
My Russian lands are not those I have known,
So too the houses and cemeteries changed, I confess.

I look around with transparency,
And see nearly everywhere
The only one for whom I care,
It is you, my sister and my friend.

You are the only one with whom I sing,
Of perfecting drawbacks of a sinner,
The song of roads was our thing
Now parting from a life of misdemeanour.

41. Would This Be the Last Time

The fog reflects blue in the snowy expanse.
A pale, waning moon shines its light.
My heart thrives in a slow, painful dance,
Remembering the bygone days and nights.

The snow on the porch starts to melt.
On a night like tonight guided by moonlight alone,
Donning my hat knowing not what I felt,
I fled from this place, my first home.

Now I've returned to that home, so dear,
But who remembers me and who forgot?
Feeling disgraced, sadly standing here
A wander who sees more travelling he wants not.

Clenching a new hat, I silently stand
Thinking how I like the sable no more
When suddenly I think of grandma and granddad
Buried under snow in the cemetery so poor.

Things are calm now, for in time we will be there,
So pointless to attempt to turn back the clock,
So this is the reason I deeply care
I have so much love for my human flock.

Nearly bursting in tears, I pondered,
And with forced smile, I wait in the fog.
Would this be the last time, I wondered,
That I see this house, this porch, and this dog?

42. Blue Is the Night

The night is a startling blue, and shows the bright
moon,
Once so young and handsome, gone so soon.

So alluring, singular, and distinct
All flies...becomes distant...extinct.

Cold beats my heart and blurry my sight...
Blue now is happiness! Moonlit the nights.

43. The Snow-Clad Plain

The snow-clad plain, the brilliant white moon,
Shrouding the lovely country side this night,
Veiled in that white, birches cry for all to see.
Who died here? Who? Could it really be me?

44. Fall Not, My Little Star

Fall not, sweet star, continue your shining,
Shine down on earth your cold rays of light,
No heart beats here in your light so blinding,
Just beyond the cemetery site.

In August you beam and bring us summer
Feeding the fields to make rye and hay,
And with the tremor and clamour,
From cranes who've chosen to stay.

Raising my face, i listen to hear
Sounds reaching from beyond the hill
A tender, sweet song about the land so dear,
Our homeland, that inspires such a thrill!

With heavy heart, the times now draws near,
No one to blame, for there's no offense.
As is bound to occur, I will someday finally rest here,
Buried below the lowly, little fence.

The gentle flame will one day be quenched
My heart will return to a ash, but worse,
Friends will leave a stone or a sad little bench,
With lively inscriptions written in verse.

The tender flame will soon die out,
My heart will turn to dust, but worse,
My fiends will place a stone, no doubt.
With words of merriment, in verse.

But, feeling grief and seeing proper,
I'd phrase it in this strange way:
He loved his homeland like a toper
Adores a bar and a buffet.

45. A Three Horse Sleigh

The snow whirls brisk and strong,
A three horse sleigh dashes along.

Some young ones ring in the sleigh for the fun.
What of my happiness? Is my joy now done?

Everything has slipped by so brisk in this way,
Dashing on through as in a three horse sleigh.

46. My Dear Old House

The snowdrift stands so fragile and callous,
Cold shines the moon from its birch at great height.
Once again I am back at my old house,
Looking through the snow storm I can see the light.

Though homeless, we no longer suffer.
Loving at last what I've got, I won't complain.
Sitting in my parent's home eating supper,
Deep is the joy to see my mother again.

Her looks sad, and I see in her eyes tears,
Silently crying, as if the world was right.
As she reaches for her tea her hand appears
To tremble, the cup slips from our sight.

My dear old mom, so gentle, you are my best,
No friends you make with this gloomy reflection.
Hear now my song, it is one of a tempest,
And know my life's story and introspection.

So much I've beheld, so much I've travelled,
Much have I loved, much have I suffered.
I have caroused, caused trouble, and unravelled,
From this poor life you make me feel buffered.

Removing worn shoes and sad little jacket,
Warming myself by the bedside at last.
I have revived with all that is good,
My hope springs up new, like in early years past.

Outside the blizzard wails and it sobs,
In a wild, noisy dance snow whirls through the night.
With such sounds it seems to be doing its job,
Removing the leaves from the lime-tress outside.

47. Don't Torment Me

Don't torment me, so stiff and so cold,
Don't ask me my years, too many I've known,
And now most grievously ill, I am told,
With my soul dry wilted, like an old yellow bone.

Years ago I was not this way.
I was dreamy and imagined a life
Of fortune, of fame, a life of all play.
Loved by all, I would never have strife.

I'm excessively rich, this is true.
My hat resting there I never will use.
I have one shirt and a worn pair of shoes,
That used to be elegant when they were new.

Fame, that I also acquired by now,
From Moscow to Paris I am well known.
My name makes people's heads bow,
Then throw them back cursing the life I have sown.

And would you not say love is amusing?
As I kiss you, your lips feel so dead.
Love I once had, I now seem to be losing,
Whereas yours bloom is still being fed.

'Tis true at times I fall gloomy – I don't care
For it too early to be so aggrieved.
The hills tender grass is so like your hair,
Rustling gold, too beautiful to believe.

I would like to be in that place,
So I might recline in the swaying grass,
Falling asleep and sinking in that space,
To daydream like a child; to let time pass.

But the things of my dreams
Are quite new to the world,
Cannot be expressed or ever be seen,
No names to express what it is that I mean.

48. Little House with Light Blue Shutters

Lowly house covered in light blue shutters,
I will never forget you, not for a day -
All these years that have gone with a stutter
Are shadowed, but feel not so far away.

Up 'til now I've dreamt of our fields
Surrounded by woods and clouds up high
Under the grey cotton shroud it yields
To the sad northern sky.

No, I cannot admire it; however
I don't want to get lost in its folds.
Perhaps what I have now is forever
The bleak warmth of a Russian soul.

In fondness I watch the silver cranes
Flying by. I don't know where they roam,
For here they can't find enough on these plains
Of ample grains to call this place home.

These cranes have known flowering trees,
Beheld brittle willows, bending and bare,
They recognize the shrill whistles of thieves
That drive them to flight with a scare.

So I cannot help being caring and proud,
My land, it is with unthinking devotions.
Covered in a worn cotton-like shroud
Deepest adoration wins over other emotions.

So very like shadows
Are those youthful days...
Lowly house covered in light blue shutters,
I will never forget you, not for a day.

49. Fields of Wheat That Shine Like Gold at Night

We move so slowly so far away
To repose in a country of peace and grace.
Maybe soon I shall have to go my way
Collect my mortal's things and to dawn face.

Oh how lovely this beech tree grove so like a picture!
Dearest Earth! And my sandy plains!
Before this host, each a mortal creature,
I cannot conceal these yearning pains.

So full I am of love and admiration
Of all that it is within the soul.
In a world of lovely aspen, lost in contemplation,
Both mind and branches reaching to foreign shoals.

Meandering through thoughts, I lose days and hours
Poems and songs I have written. And I do not grieve.
I know happiness in this dreary world of ours,
To have had such a life, so fortunately received.

My happiness complete with love's first kiss,
I've rolled through the grass and lain in a flower-bed.
And to decency and kindness I am not remiss,
For I've never beaten an animal bout the head.

Unknown lands know not such a blooming picture,
They lack the fields of wheat so divine,
Before this host, each a mortal creature,
Sends shivers down my human spine.

Outside this country they will never know
The fields of wheat shining brilliant at night.
It is the reason why I choose not to go,
But rather to live on this warm country-side.

50. I Will Not Be Wandering Out

You will not find me wandering out
Plodding goosefoot in the bushes now;
And I must accept that you won't turn about
Oat-haired in my dreams with your vow.

Back then you were tender, gorgeous, fair,
So like sweet juice your bright white skin,
When blushing you were like a sun's flare,
Shining on the snow, so lustrous you have been.

Now you appear to shed your light, your eyes fade,
And time has slowly eroded the sound of you name.
But buried with the folds of you shawl is still laid
The sweet honey smell of loves lost game.

During the quiet hour as sunset shines,
So like a kitten cleaning its face,
I hear the hive-like water sing the lines
Singing sweet songs of you to space.

Let me whisper some to the evening blue,
How you're a dream or divine song.
After all, who designed that waist for you?
Someone who knew a holy secret all along?

Having shed their grain your eyes are fading,
And your name melts like the sound of chimes;
But the folders of your crumpled shawl and veiling
Hold the honey smell from your arms like vines.

51. Jubilant Adolescence

Leaves are falling all around.
And the wind
Drawls so low.
Who can my heart make happily bound?
Who can soothe me, my friend, do you know?

I stare at the moon, fighting sleep,
Striving to keep the drowsiness away.
There the roosters aloud crying keep
All aware of the dawning of another day.

Early hours of day light, blue forever...
Blissful joy, the stars fly with grace...
So many wishes I should now make. However,
For wishes I have no starting place.

I know not what to wish for now,
Cursing home, my fate, the world?
What I dearly want, I vow,
Is by my window a pretty girl.

My desire for her,
As an exception,
Is that she convey that her only need is me,
And with most tender words of affection,
To bring peace to my soul so fondly.

Once I can accept these lessons,
On such a glorious moonlit night
I might not melt and faint from delight,
And with jubilant adolescence,
Be well pleased that my youth is right.

52. With a Humble Heart

As if in a smoke filled room, you hide from view.
With a weakened heart I must pray for you.

Your nurturing image nourishes my soul,
My one and all, you fill my heart's hole.

The world awash in the sun's glorious flame,
It is here eternal truth lives with no name.

Consider the dream kept by time,
Through you they have seeds most sublime.

Unseen words grow in such an arable plot,
Mingled with feathery grass without a thought.

Held up high by strong upraised hands,
The sound wakens churches in surrounding lands.

There are souls that take delight in crushing your
glow,
Following your tracks in the new fallen snow.

But the beauty and gentles of faded zeal
Of ones such as you are lovelier still.

53. The Gate of Paradise

A silver road,
Do you call me anew?
As a fiery candle's load,
Burns so brightly over you.

Does your warm stem from joy or sorrow?
Or is insanity your intent?
My heart, my soul, help me past tomorrow
To love this hard snow to my end.

Give me sunset for this sleigh
Willow branch lovely in the ice.
Maybe after my final day
I'll reach the gate of paradise.

54. My Heart in Its Sorrowful Glory

No, I've yet to forget you, my sweet,
The hair's bright shine and beauty deep.
It was not easy, nor was it pleasant
When you I left; it made we weep.

I still remember those autumn nights,
And the gentle rustle of birches;
The days seemed shorter, the sun less bright,
The moon shared less time in the sky's perches.

It was then you whispered sad words in my ear:
"These wonderful years and dreams will be gone,
When you choose to go with another (I know and fear),
And leave me along, though it is wrong."

That lime proudly standing in bloom,
Refreshes strong love anew,
I remember how, before this doom,
I showered beautiful flowers on you.

My heart in its sorrowful glory,
Carries fond remembrance of you,
My friend, as in a fanciful story,
It was in love my heart then grew.

55. My Life

It appears my life is fated for the worst;
My way is all paved with trouble and distress.
Severed from play, all fun will burst,
Sorrow and wounds will always afflict my chest.

It has proved so far I'm fated to suffer from pain.
My life is full of the worst misfortune and luck.
Still early in life I've suffered time and again
Both body and soul no torture have ducked.

The future makes promise of wonderful joy,
But sighs and tears have been my only solutions.
As the storm looms and begins, to fate I'm a toy,
And will be ruined by those illustrious illusions.

Though I now know life's lowly deception,
I complain not of this wretched disaster.
While my soul suffers not from grief and affliction,
There is no rescue from this life-fated master.

56. Farewell, my friend, farewell

Farewell my friend, farewell;
My dearest one, you're in my heart.
The predetermined parting from above,
Will reunite us later and we'll never part.

Farewell, my friend, don't speak, don't shake my hand;
Please don't despair and don't frown your brow.
To perish in this life is nothing novel,
Although to live, of course, is also nothing new.

17811908R00040

Printed in Great Britain
by Amazon